# FIX YOU,
# FIX YOUR DOG

## PALMETTO
### PUBLISHING
Charleston, SC
www.PalmettoPublishing.com

Paperback ISBN: 9798822924024
eBook ISBN: 979-8-8229-2403-1

# FIX YOU,
# FIX YOUR DOG

## EMILY ADAMS

# Introduction

# MY STORY

I was born in 1989 in Oceanside, California. I did most of my growing up in Twentynine Palms, California, where my dad was stationed in the military for a while. We then moved to a little town called Yucca Valley, California, where I lived until I turned seventeen and then ventured out to the East Coast.

I remember my first dog: a golden retriever we named Cassie. I was twelve years old, and my parents had finally agreed to let me have a dog. It was funny because, when I was younger, I was petrified of dogs. I had a fear of them for no known reason, and I would go into panic attacks from the noise of a jingling collar or the sight of a trotting dog. I guess some things we really do just outgrow.

I was the nerdy kid who went to the library to study up on dog-training books, and I sat in our garage every day reading all the tips and tricks to being a great trainer and how to train my dog. These lessons were, of course, put to practice on Cassie, and

I enjoyed taking her to obedience classes in our local areas, learning and studying with the trainers there.

My first gig as a professional dog trainer was when I moved to the East Coast and got hired at PetSmart. I started training just two days a week because they already had their full-time trainers. During this time, I was attending animal behavior college, where I was learning the basic principles of classical and operant conditioning. I was paired with a mentor and got to work with many different types of dogs while still holding my training job at PetSmart. Before graduating from animal behavior college, I was already hired by my mentor to run and conduct their group obedience classes at Kellar's Canine Academy in Saddle Brooke, New Jersey. I was now instructing classes for both Kellar's and PetSmart while visiting my own clients at their homes for one-on-one sessions. At PetSmart, I quickly began being asked to step into other trainers' classes to help coach and assist if they had "problem dogs" they were stumped on. I was signing people up for my classes like a true salesperson and became the only trainer in the district with the number of sales and full classes I was giving. I also built a reputation for what they called "rollover classes." These were classes that would continue after the first courses the owners took and developed a good clientele and following, to the point where I never finished a group class and didn't get clients to continue. Managers soon took notice, and I eventually became the only full-time trainer for that store.

I was then asked by my district to coach and help other trainers learn to do the same, and I went out to other stores in other areas, giving seminars and sharing what I was doing and why I was successful. After five years of training at PetSmart and three years at Kellar's Canine Academy, I witnessed an unmet need for "problem dogs" that neither PetSmart nor other competitors could assist in dealing with. Their curriculum was very basic and did not offer things like aggression work. But somehow, I attracted client after client who needed help with their dog's aggression or behavioral issues that the common dog-training companies were not suitable for. I was now training full time at Kellar's Canine Academy and shuffling my full-time gig at PetSmart. I started studying, planning, and dreaming of my own company where any dog could come and be helped no matter the problems they were encountering. I wanted to serve as the area's training camp that took on any dog and turned away no one. I saw too many dog owners leaving these places distraught, feeling hopeless after we had had to turn them away, and this inspired me to become an entrepreneur and open my own training camp.

By June 2016, I was ready to take on this daunting task of running my own dog-training company. Due to the company's noncompete contract, I had to quit my training job at PetSmart, where I had worked for five years.

While I ran private classes out of people's homes and local parks, I decided to find a job somewhere without a noncompete contract to wait out my contract at PetSmart while still getting to train. I was hired at a local Petco store in Hackensack, and before their schooling was over, I was already teaching their groups and private lessons. I built up another clientele there, and the clients would soon be customers for life.

In 2017, my new company, K9 Boot Camp, was born. We quickly became the area's best-known training camp for dog training and behavior. Training over four hundred dogs a year and profiting by our second year in business, K9 Boot Camp won best dog trainers of the area from the East Rutherford awards program three years in a row. We were honored with the Bergen County success award from the SBDC for our outstanding takeoff and growth in such a short time frame. As the company grew bigger, I sought out other mentors in coaching and behavioral training but also in business ownership. It was all new to me. After all, I was just a young girl in my twenties, learning and growing with something so big and so fast that I couldn't keep up at times. I studied e-collar work and training at the amazing K9 Connection in Buffalo, New York, with Tyler Muto. I then met a teacher I would work with for the next four years: Andres Aportella at Pro Canine Center.

The first case he was brought on for was a case I'll never forget. It changed my name from just a great trainer to one of the best. It put K9 Boot Camp on the map for treating aggression cases and offering outstanding obedience performance. The dog was named Ferdinand. Ferdinand had a bad association with small children and couldn't see them from even a hundred feet away without going into a full-blown aggression explosion at the end of the leash. I was taught all about reading the dog's body and signals, how to work with thresholds, and driving aggression out. This dog ended the training program by being able to walk by a group of children, pass traffic after school, and see the school bus let out many children, all while keeping a calm, cool composure. You'd never know he had a problem with aggression around children. After this was posted on the company's website and social platforms, calls came in like hurricanes. Everyone was willing to pay a higher price. Everyone wanted to be a part of K9 Boot Camp, and everyone had respect for the company and what it was accomplishing. Something so different from what was typically offered at your regular day-to-day training companies. K9 Boot Camp lasted five years, until the town decided we kenneled too many noisy barking dogs in the area we were in, which did not suit the nearby apartment complexes. We had grown so massively that our training facility was no longer big enough for all the business and dogs that were coming in. We had sixty-five dogs in the training center at one time and maxed out the center's capacity by year three. The dogs we took in were usually dogs with severe aggression or behavioral issues that got them sent away from most other places prior; K9 Boot Camp became the neighborhood's magnet for the bad dogs. So, of course, dogs coming in would be unruly and wild—and the barking! With sixty-five dogs all in a kennel, could you expect anything else? But the town was done with it after five years, and K9 Boot Camp came to its end.

I now work with clients one-on-one, traveling to their homes for consults and lessons and taking on behavioral cases for boarding and training at home. Emily's name and reputation as the "female Cesar Milan" extended beyond the Bergen County, New Jersey, area and have spread throughout the East Coast. She continues to get requests from dog owners who struggle with their dogs and haven't had success elsewhere. Emily is in the process of creating a dog-training facility that, rather than a kennel, provides a homelike environment for dogs in training programs. This will create a more comfortable atmosphere and avoid the stress of a shelter-like kennel.

I have two German shepherds, a working dog, Tundra, and my beloved Jericho. Tundra was titled in BH and IGP 1, and Jericho won second place in highest scoring for BH. I have earned certifications from many organizations, including the CPDT-KA, ABCDT level 1 and ABCDT level 2, and the CGC instructor certification from the American Kennel Club, and continue to grow and learn in the dog-training world.

While life takes us through many journeys and changes, I will probably always do training in some shape or form. I love the spirit of the dog. The true honesty and loyalty they teach us are unparalleled to any other species we encounter on our planet. I strive to help people better understand and learn about our cherished canine companions, and I'm blessed to be the vessel of communication between dogs and their owners. This book provides the foundations and basics for getting you started on the right foot when owning a new dog or already owning a dog you're struggling with in basic manners or general questions about your dog's training. Each chapter is set up to be its own guide, so feel free to skip chapters, come back to chapters, and read the ones that are most helpful to you as you will learn the fundamental lessons in those certain subjects you choose. I hope you enjoy this book as much as I enjoyed writing it for you.

Happy training,

*Emily Adams*

# Chapter 1

# THE ART OF TETHERING

All too often, when I visit people's homes, I am greeted by a bouncing, mouthy, and wild little puppy. The harried owner will usually ask, "How do we stop this?" or "Why is she like this?" The simple answer is that too much freedom was given to the puppy at a young age. The puppy is free to roam the house, leap up onto the counters, devour eyeglasses and toilet paper like food at a buffet, and run rampant through his domain, a veritable party house playground. The owners will often tell me all about the expensive furniture, shoes, or prescription glasses that have become casualties of a canine tornado. When a puppy has been allowed since a young age to "free roam the home," he has learned that this is acceptable behavior. And who was his teacher? YOU!

It can be a tough situation, but the great news is that you can *unteach* your dog what you have already taught it. By having a simple (non-bulky) collar and an attached—yes, attached—leash, you can teach your young pup boundaries and manners within the home. How many times do you see a service animal jumping all over and pulling its owner? A show of hands, please. That's right, when we see service animals, they are usually unfazed by distractions, calmly lying at their owner's feet while their owners get to enjoy a meal at an outdoor restaurant or coffee at their favorite little home away from home. The service animal seems like everyone's dream pet. "Why can't my dog be calm like that?" I often hear dog owners lament. The answer, my friend, is simple: tethering.

Now, when I say tethering, I'm not talking about tying the dog up all day. Far from it. This simply means you have a leash on your dog when they are young to teach them boundaries. If I'm watching TV, I can have my dog lying at my feet while I hold her leash so that she can learn to lie down on the floor while I sit on the furniture and enjoy a TV show. If I wasn't holding the leash, my dog would be free to roam about. Not needing me for anything.

She could find fun messes like bathroom shampoo bottles, towels, or toilet paper. She could be counter surfing for food or scraps from your last dinner. Tethering simply means keeping your dog with you at the end of the leash to ensure you can keep an eye on your dog and supervise its activities. This is how your dog learns manners, just like your favorite well-behaved service dog. When service dogs were puppies being raised and trained to assist people with disabilities, they weren't taken to dog parks or let loose inside the home. They were taught the art of tethering. They learned to stay in proximity to their owners; they learned boundaries and manners within the home. This, in turn, transferred to their way of behaving when outside and in the public eye.

As your puppy progresses through the tethering method, you can start to allow a little more independence, but the puppy should still be dragging the leash. You're not holding on to it anymore, but you can certainly grab it if you need to correct, coach, or communicate a wrong choice the puppy makes. You can quickly grab the leash to go outside for potty breaks, too, without the hassle of harnessing up the dog each time. We'll talk more about potty training in the next chapter.

# Chapter 2

# MY POTTY TRAINING SECRETS 101

When I got my first puppy, I was twelve years old, and my parents wanted our dog to be trained to use the bathroom in a certain area of the yard only. A designated spot so that we would not have to wander the yard looking for feces. Later, when I got my first dog as an adult and had my own place, a small apartment, and then my second dog in a large house, different potty training concepts and protocols applied to each different living situation. In this chapter, we will go over proper potty training techniques and which ones will likely work best for you and your current living situation.

Remember in chapter 1 how we talked about how tethering provides better supervision and management? The tethering concept applies to first-time potty training habits as well. Too much free roaming means more accidents and more places all over the home. If you keep your dog on a leash with you during the potty training phase, this can prevent unnecessary accidents and unwanted habits from forming.

## *Potty Training for Small Spaces Like Apartments or Small Condos*

If you're in a small apartment or condo, you probably have an elevator or lots of steps. In this case, when taking the puppy out, because waiting for an elevator can be lengthy, *carry* the puppy outside! Puppies rarely eliminate in your arms while being carried. If you walk them down the hallway and wait for the elevator, then that one is full, so you wait on another—there's your accident! If you hold the puppy while waiting, this is less likely to happen. The moment you get outside, put your puppy down and let him or her start to sniff around.

Brining sprays that smell like puppies' urine or finding spots where other dogs have previously peed can help. Sometimes it doesn't. Every puppy is different. You will need to learn your own puppy's habits and signals. You also want to be mindful of getting a new puppy in locations where it's cold in the wintertime. So many clients of mine have complaints about having to go out in the cold. Who told you to get a puppy in the winter? If you do, this is something you need to prepare for, as you will be going out as often as every hour or every thirty minutes, depending on the breed, temperament, and age. When in small apartments or condos, we are also forced to walk more than if we had a huge backyard where we could just open the door and let the dog go out. Multiple walks in a day are healthy, not only for exercise and tiring the puppy out but also for social skills and learning.

## *Potty Training for Bigger Houses or Yards*

When you have a bigger house or yard space where your dog can be let out, this saves you from having to carry your puppy, waiting on elevators, or going up and down forty-plus stairs multiple times a day! This doesn't mean your puppy shouldn't get walked, but it is a lot easier on the potty training program. Please be mindful of things like doggy doors for younger puppies and young adults who do not yet have manners or formal training. Providing puppies free access to something so wonderful as a big back-yard—allowing them to access it without needing you, bolt out the doors, and not learn to politely exit and enter thresholds—can work against you later on. Save doggy doors for the trained, more mature dogs that have already learned manners and respect for you and the household and are 110 percent pot-ty trained before considering something like a doggy door. If you have a large yard, you may want to teach your puppy to only eliminate in a specific spot so that you are not wandering the massive yard having to find the feces to clean. To do this, simply take the puppy out on a leash and bring them to the desired designated spot. Don't let them walk all over when trying to go; instead, let them sniff in an area sort of like a square or circle of five feet. Once they eliminate in that designated spot, it never hurts to pay up with a special treat! After doing this for a while, your puppy will be in the habit of finding his toilet area on his own.

## *Potty Training Bible*

I always tell my clients about the puppy potty-log bible! This can be any notebook or notepad kept anywhere that's easily accessible to you. What you do is keep a log of the day, time, and where the puppy eliminated. For example, if your puppy pees at 2:15 p.m. on the carpet while you're in the shower, log that! Over the next five days or so, you can start to see your puppy's patterns. For example, you can start to see that your puppy specifically seems to pee within forty-five minutes after eating, fifteen minutes after a play session, or after drinking water. The potty training bible will let you know the schedule so you are not guessing and going outside one hundred times a day when your puppy may not even need to go. To keep from guessing, log your puppy's habits, whether they eliminated in the yard, outside on a walk, or in the home and made an accident. Everything can be logged to help you determine your puppy's habits and scheduling needs.

Next, control the food and water. Do not leave water out for the puppy to freely access at random times throughout the day. You will never have a schedule this way, and you will never find the rhyme or reason for when your puppy is going to have an accident! If you know that after fifteen minutes of drinking water, your puppy usually needs to pee, and you know you gave your puppy water at 2:00 p.m., then you know around 2:15 p.m. your puppy should probably be brought outside to potty. You can also see how much your puppy drank, or if he drank at all. If the water is left out all day, you may not see when your puppy is drinking or how much. This means you'll have accidents in the home, and you'll forever guess when to take them outside.

Some breeds of dogs can handle fewer feeding times throughout the day. For example, if your dog eats three meals a day, one cup each time, you can break this down to one and a half cups twice a day or three cups once a day, depending on the potty training needs. If my puppy was the type that need-ed to go out every fifteen to thirty minutes at eight weeks old, I certainly would want to reduce the three meals—that's a lot of taking out to do! Especially if you are in the elevator situation. If you have a big-ger breed puppy and you're feeding larger amounts to limit the meal count, make sure to feed with a slow-feeder bowl or a wobbler or puzzle toy to slow down the gulping or swallowing of air.

It's always a good idea to reward your puppy with a treat of their liking anytime they eliminate in the designated spot. It never hurts to pay up!

## Crate Training for Potty Training

A lot of doggy owners ask me if they need a crate during potty training. The answer is always yes, and here is why: When you are potty training, the idea is to train the puppy to hold it for longer and longer, slowly increasing the puppy's ability to wait to relieve itself. In a lot of cases, owners tell me they take the puppy out and go for long walks, only to come back inside and watch the puppy pee or poop on their carpet or rug.

First, if the puppy didn't go outside, why bring them back in and let them off the leash to make the accident? Put them in a crate for another few minutes (the time depends on your dog), and then put the leash back on and go right back outside to try again. You don't have to take another lengthy walk. You can instead just stand in an area of a few feet and let the puppy roam and sniff around that area. If she doesn't go, she's brought back to the crate to hold it, and then we try again. If the puppy DOES go outside and eliminate during this potty break, THEN go for a walk. So now you are allowing the puppy to get the walk after he's done his business. Not only does this help teach the puppy to go to the bathroom immediately when brought outside (in case you can't go for a long walk), but it also helps you not have to walk forty-five minutes EVERY potty break. To help eliminate more "guessing" and more "potty breaks," keep your potty journal or potty training bible logs accurate so you know exactly the timing and requirements for YOUR individual puppy and won't have to guess when to go out.

If you don't have a crate to put the puppy in, you will always have to carry them or keep them on a leash with you until the elimination has occurred outside. You will notice it's less of a struggle to have a safe spot to put them where you know they will not have accidents. Now what if your puppy eliminates in the crate? You want to check a few things that may be the reason for this. First, is the crate too big? You don't want so much room that the puppy can pee or poop in one corner and then easily escape it and go sleep comfortably in the opposite corner. You want the crate only big enough, at this stage, for the puppy to stand up, turn around, and lie down. If they eliminate in it, they won't have enough room to escape it, and therefore they learn it's not so cozy to sit in their own feces.

Another tip: don't leave food and water in the crate. Your designated feeding times should apply. Another reason they may be having accidents in the crate is because they have a soft blanket or towel to absorb whenever they pee! Don't put cloth or bedding in a young puppy's crate while potty training. They should be sleeping or staying on the plastic tray that comes with most crates. Most crates come with a divider so that you can make the crate small during potty training days and then take it out to make a bigger crate as the puppy grows into an adult. This saves you from having to buy another crate when your dog is an adult.

# Chapter 3

# KIRA—MY BEST TEACHER

Kira. My precious Kira. Kira was a Siberian husky and rottweiler mix. She had beautiful blue eyes, ears that stood straight up like a German shepherd, and a silky, fluffy black coat. Kira was given her name for its meaning: "gift from God," and oh, she was.

Before I met Kira, I experienced a very difficult situation, having to give away my sick Labrador retriever mix by the name of Nadia, whom I had rescued. She had been my dog from the time she was a puppy, but she eventually developed parvovirus upon delivery and later struggled with demodectic mange. Nadia's vet care eventually became something that was out of my reach after having stripped every credit card of their funds to pay for her medical treatment to survive parvo. When the mange got bad enough, I realized she would not be able to survive much longer without the expensive treatment needed. I was no longer able to care for Nadia's medical needs. A kind and beautiful soul at the medical facility where Nadia was being treated offered to become Nadia's new owner and give her all the medical help she would need at no cost. It was obvious that I would have to let go of Nadia if I wanted her to live. I knew this was best for her. Nadia and I said goodbye that day, and she was taken off to start her treatment and her new life.

After experiencing the loss of my best friend, I didn't think I was ready for another dog just yet. At that time, I was training for a corporate client, and I walked by a customer with a shopping cart full of brand-new husky-rottweiler puppies. The customer was shopping for supplies while the blue-eyed beauties sat in her rattling shopping carriage. I asked her if there was anything I could assist her with (as an excuse to see the puppies). My favorite was a little black one that seemed to be the queen of the litter and who took quite a keen interest in me. "Oh! she is adorable!" I commented, only to get the unexpected response of "She's yours if you want her." Rather shocked and in disbelief, all I could muster was an excited "What?" The customer replied, "They're free—my dog had an unplanned litter, and I'm looking for a good home for each of the puppies." This is how I became Fatty Mama's new owner—later named Kira. She was not only given to me as a gift when I had lost someone so precious to me, but the life lessons she would eventually teach me would be the biggest gift of all. While Kira taught me many valuable lessons, for the sake of this book, I will mention two specific events that changed my dog-training career and my understanding of dogs in general for the better.

## *Lesson 1: Training Methods*

On a very beautiful and sunny Wednesday, Kira and I decided to venture into her favorite park in Bergen County, New Jersey. It was a very large park with a lot of activity and owners who would walk their dogs around a big, beautiful lake with seemingly endless floating ducks. I specifically took Kira here to work on training exercises because of the park's ample, spacious fields. On this day, we were going to practice Kira's recall, where I called her, and she had to come back to me no matter the distractions or the activities going on around her.

Kira's favorite treat was string cheese, and I had brought a few sticks to work on her recall. The more distractions you have, the better the reward should be, right? Well, it was during this particular training session that Kira saw her favorite prey: squirrels. Of course, a squirrel decided to dart out in front of Kira, creating a rambunctious game of chase. Kira's leash detached, and she managed to run right through and out of the leash. The squirrel was running straight toward the busy street, and, inevitably, so was Kira.

Cars were coming and going, and Kira was getting too far from me. I was calling her name, repeating her recall command "come," while waving cheese and running in the opposite direction to encourage her to chase me rather than the squirrel. After all, this is exactly what I was taught to do in situations like this by most of my then-teachers in the positive dog-training world. "Positive dog training" is the title in America given to dog training where the trainer solely depends on food motivation to get the dog to comply with their commands. As Kira bolted off after the squirrel with all her hunt and prey instincts in full force, I realized I had failed miserably. If it weren't for a tree that the squirrel ran up, I would have never gotten ahold of Kira.

It was this day and this moment that I realized if Kira or any dog was more motivated by something else, like the fast squirrel, then their desire to listen when training would fail. I would later learn from a very good teacher of mine that if your dog was trained via food motivation only, your dog did nothing wrong in this scenario. I was, of course, the one at fault. My teacher said to me, "You have taught your dog to listen only when motivated. Your dog was never committed to your training, and she never learned responsibility to the master." Instead, she learned to go after whatever was pleasing and rewarding for her in that moment. And at that time, Kira's desire to chase her favorite prey—squirrels—outweighed a cheap piece of cheese by a long shot. That was the event that changed my perception of what real dog training was and was not. What real dog training meant and what results could actually be accomplished.

From this day forward, for the next seven years, I would study with the same teacher: a great dog master by the name of Andres Aportella. I studied what most might call "compulsion training," "balanced training," or "training through simulation." Call it what you want. I learned what it meant to have a dog trained in what my teacher called "responsibility to the master." Once I began to adopt not only food and motivational training but also add other methods and techniques I learned, I started seeing dogs with full-turnaround success stories. Dogs with severe dog-to-dog reactivity or dogs with extreme leash aggression became dogs that could walk by another dog with ease and not explode when visitors came into their homes. I witnessed firsthand a 100 percent turnaround and unimaginable results. If it hadn't been for Kira's incident with the squirrel, I would have never sought out better training or learned just how limited food motivation training by itself could be in the world of dog training.

Sure, we can use rewards like food treats and toys to *motivate* and *reinforce* good behaviors, but we must ask ourselves: What about discipline? Do we not discipline our children? Are there no consequences for us when we speed? We get speeding tickets, have to pay fines, and so on. We aren't just rewarded when we drive the speed limit then ignored when we don't, as they so often teach in positive-only training.

E-collars and prong collars—when used properly and under the guidance of a professional—can be the best training tools for dogs who struggle with behavioral issues, or "not listening" as we often call it. My training approach is no longer limited to only one approach. Instead, I use balancing approaches to cover all corners of training, which is far more than what your food-alone approach may provide.

It's also worth mentioning that not every dog even cares about food. Most trainers offering solely food training will say, "Your dogs should be rehomed," "His aggression is too much for me to handle," or "I'm not experienced enough to handle this dog." These are all quite common statements clients make when getting "difficult dogs." If your one approach doesn't work, I have a toolbox of experience, tools, and techniques that allow me to help almost any dog owner and their dog with any problem. If you're limited in your training approach, your results will also remain limited.

## *Lesson 2: Dealing with Separation Anxiety*

In the fall of 2013, Kira and I were faced with a moving challenge. I was on a mission to find a place of my own. No roommates. No basements. I wanted an apartment that I could fully afford by myself but would also accept a dog of Kira's breed and size. My lease was up at my old place, and it would take some time to find the right place for Kira and me. I had the option to stay with a friend and keep Kira with me there for a few months until we found my permanent home. Unfortunately, the landlord there found out she was housing us, and we were instructed to leave. I then took Kira to work with me when possible and dropped her off at many different friends' places during days when she could not come to work with me. Every time I left Kira with a friend, she would look back at me as they took her away, and she started resisting me leaving her. She would pull them toward me and my car as they tried to steer away. This would turn into her two-year struggle with separation anxiety.

While Kira did not seem to exhibit separation anxiety when left at friends' houses, she was not adapting too well to being left in our new place, completely alone, when I left for work. Kira developed separation anxiety so severe that she would chew herself bloody, pace back and forth for hours while howling like a wolf to the moon, and drool excessively until my return. There was one day I came home from work and found her frozen, shaking, and bloody in a corner of my apartment, which is when I realized something was terribly wrong. This was a serious condition and not something she would just outgrow or get over. My dog was suffering and struggling to be left alone without me.

I didn't know much about the term "separation anxiety" but came to learn it was very common for huskies. Kira was especially susceptible given her history of being left alone so many times in different places during our moving situation, not knowing how or when I would be returning for her. I began to seek out separation anxiety specialists and dog behaviorists. I bought every book that touched on the subject of separation anxiety. I soon learned that I could read all the books out there on the subject but would still need to work with a behaviorist as I was in over my head. This, in turn, taught me all the ins and outs of how to help dogs who had or developed separation anxiety.

I found a behavioralist, and our first visit was three hours for $750. I had saved up for weeks just to be able to pay for the first visit. Kira and I continued working with this behaviorist for the next six months and then carried out the training protocols for the next two years. When Kira first developed separation anxiety, I could not go as far as across the street to buy a half- gallon of milk without returning to a distraught, confused, and emotionally unwell friend. I learned that when working with separation anxiety, you cannot or should not leave your dog past a time that pushes them to the point where they feel any distress because this can backtrack the progress. Therefore, I knew I would have to have a team in place. I hired a walker, dog sitter, backup sitter, and day care to ensure that whatever life would bring me, Kira was assured to never be left alone. Once my team was in place and everyone was on our planned schedule, I started the counter-conditioning process.

During this process, you present the triggers that indicate to your dog that you are leaving, and you then undo these meanings. For example, grabbing my car keys, my purse, or my coat were all signs to Kira that I was planning on leaving. The time of day also matters. You must undo that association too. So, at sixty-five reps a day and nine different time slots throughout the day, I would randomly pick up my car keys just to set them back down. I would wake up at 4:00 a.m., get dressed for work, take my clothes back off, and go back to sleep. I would start my car just to turn it back off and come back inside. These all helped to recondition Kira's mind and allow these triggers to lose their meaning to her over time.

I also made sure Kira was properly exercised before leaving; when she was tired, it could sometimes help lessen her anxiety. We went on a thirty-minute bike ride anytime before I left. She was then left with all kinds of puzzle toys throughout the house with high-value treats to keep her mind occupied. I would leave for just ten seconds before the sitter would walk in and stay with her. Yes, just ten seconds is what Kira could handle at the beginning, and that's where we started. From ten seconds, we worked our way up to a full two hours within eight months. After two full years of counter conditioning, paying a team, working with a behavioralist, and having a strict exercise plan in place, Kira was finally able to adapt and live a life where she could be home alone in no distress, and I was free to come and go as I pleased once more.

A lot of people along the way told me, "You could always rehome her to a family who's home all the time," "Maybe she's not a good fit for you," or "This is too much to work around." So on and so forth. Of course, it was a huge life adjustment and inconvenience, but I knew in my heart that Kira needed *me* to help fix this problem. If not me, who else would do it for her? I loved Kira, and I didn't want to give up on her.

To this day, I am paid top dollar to help clients whose dogs have separation anxiety, and I have Kira to thank. I've helped treat dogs with this problem who had it so bad that they would try to jump out of eight-story buildings in order to get to their owners. They can now live a peaceful life at home alone. Would I have ever tiptoed into the subject of separation anxiety if not for Kira? Would I have learned so much about the issue if I hadn't worked with a professional? Probably not. Perhaps I would never have become a behavioralist myself if I hadn't worked so closely with one during Kira's treatment plan.

When trying to help a dog with separation anxiety, first you need to determine how long they can be alone without any distress. Start there. Next, you must determine how to make a lesson plan to fit your daily schedule. Hire a team like I did, or if you work from home, purposely schedule yourself to go out for different reasons to allow practice time for the lesson plan. Third, know or find out what your dog likes to do that is high value enough that they keep their attention on doing it even after you step out of the picture. For Kira, one of these things was a squirrel toy (go figure) that made noise and moved. It was battery powered, and it was by far the only thing that kept her attention even if I approached the door to leave. You want to set these types of toys down before leaving to entertain the dog's mind and to help break the cycle of your dog going into distress in your absence. Because of Kira's struggle and my determination to help her, today, I have saved more than forty-five dogs who were on death row because of this condition, kept hundreds of dogs in their homes, and become a knowledge-able trainer in this subject. Our dogs are our best teachers. They teach us patience and unconditional love—and that is what Kira did for me. She also kept me quite fit with all those bike rides.

# Chapter 4

# EXERCISE: PHYSICAL VERSUS MENTAL

By this point, we know that too much freedom can create an energetic and mischievous dog and that tethering is a good tool to help manage how much freedom our dog receives. We also know that crates can help with supervision and enforce boundaries. But what if, while being tethered and crate trained, your dog just will not stop chewing at his leash or at you? What if he continues to bark and act crazy while in the crate even after doing days of crate and tether training?

Let's talk about your dog's exercise. Many of the common problems I see with dogs I have trained are caused by lack of exercise—both mental and physical.

### *Physical Exercise*

Making sure your dog is getting plenty of physical exercise can help prevent and solve numerous problems that many dog owners probably wouldn't suspect. Many of us may think that physical exercise consists of taking our dogs out several times a day to eliminate or allowing our dogs to roam and sniff around the yard (which usually consists of lounging or sunbathing). These things do not actually count as physical exercise, at least not in the sense of getting enough of it. Depending on the dog's breed, age, and temperament, she may need more or less physical exercise.

While a good thirty-minute fast-paced walk is good physical exercise, try two or three! It is important to keep in mind that if your dog is walking you, stopping every few seconds to sniff around, or zigzagging from side to side, then your dog is not receiving the full benefit of physical exercise. When your dog walks you, the walk becomes less draining for your dog, and you will likely still have a hyper and energetic dog when you arrive back home.

Dogs enjoy having a job. Something that makes them feel accomplished and useful. A structured and effective walk ensures that your dog will feel this way. In chapter 5, "The Power of the Walk," I talk more about walking manners.

## *Mental Exercise*

I often hear from my clients that "I can run my dog for miles, and he still has the zoomies when we come back" or "I walk my dog several times a day for hours, and they come home even more hyper." This is likely because you have done the work of physical exercise, but your dog is lacking mental exercise. Mental exercise teaches the dog's brain to settle, to feel accomplished, and to have a job. These jobs come in many forms, from hunting their prey to obeying heeling commands while walking.

A great way to fulfill this need for mental exercise is with a puzzle toy. These toys can easily be found in pet shops and online stores. Things like the Kong Wobbler, Busy Buddy–brand toys, a stuffed frozen Kong, puzzle mazes, etc. As for the Kong Wobbler, think about when a dog hunts or when they eat their prey: they tear into it, search through it, and eat the meat they worked hard to hunt. This toy provides the same fulfillment as the dog works through it to get all the filling out. You can fill these toys with wet dog food mixed with their own kibble and freeze them. Something like yogurt with dry kibble, peanut butter, and cream cheese all work well as a Kong filler. Another easy alternative is a good chew bone. Every dog should have access to appropriate chews for their age and size. You'd be surprised at how much calmer your dog is after a good chew!

Last, but certainly not least, is the best mental stimulation of all: training. Training with your dog not only provides their mind with a great learning session and mental stimulation, but it also increases your bond with your dog as you both work together, build trust, have fun, and learn together. Training creates structure and a job for your dog. It aids in boredom and prevents a lot of problem behavior from starting or continuing. Obedience training is fundamental to a well-balanced dog. Some issues, like excessive barking, chewing, and nipping, are all solved with simple obedience drills.

### *Breakdown of a Balanced Routine:*

1. Get enough physical exercise. Step it up with a weighted backpack or treadmill. Make sure your dog isn't walking you.
2. Provide enough mental stimulation with a Kong, puzzle toy, chew bone, and training.

Now you're on your way to a healthy, balanced working team!

# Chapter 5

# THE POWER OF A WALK—A DOG NAMED SHILOH

On a very hot and humid Pennsylvania day in 2023, I was walking a dog who was staying in my board-and-train program for her extreme leash reactivity toward humans and other dogs. She became explosive and anxious at the sight of, well, anything! Her name was Shiloh. Shiloh was a little tan pit bull who, at most times, seemed to always be in fight mode. Everything seemed to set Shiloh off: me pulling on her leash, setting down her food dish, opening or closing a door, the sound of the mailman, faint voices in the distance, and even a blowing leaf. I thought to myself, "I need to figure out how to turn this dog's nervous system off!"

During our first walk together, Shiloh was pulling me so hard that she forced me to run right behind her while I continued holding onto the leash for dear life. She was zigzagging left and right, and I was on the verge of tripping over myself. Her ears, nose, and tail were going in every direction as if she were on the hunt for an invisible predator. It was evident to me that Shiloh did not know how to feel at peace even during a relaxing walk. I decided to take a step back on obedience work and just observe Shiloh, allowing her to teach me what *she* needed from *me* before I began teaching her what I needed from her.

Since I first noticed Shiloh's nervous, erratic energy during our walk, I figured further observation and understanding of her behavior could be done through going on more walks together. At first, we could not walk very far distances because everything seemed to set her off. I took her up and down the street without implementing obedience training yet, with the goal of observation. This allowed her to feel my calm energy as well as let some of that energy rub off on her. It was then that a huge garbage truck passed by us, and she bolted toward it with a low snarl and quick explosion. Out of reflex, I held up the leash with a quick jerk and told her, "No." It was then that Shiloh finally showed me what she needed: direction, instruction, input, and a guide. She looked at me with a puzzled stare as if to say, "I don't need to react like this?" For the entire rest of the walk, she kept checking in on me, looking at me as if I were her new leader. She seemed at peace, and her mind was quiet, perhaps for the first time in her life.

Now that Shiloh and I had a better understanding of one another, we soon started our anti-pull and focus drills during our walks together. We were still only walking up and down my street, but we had gotten somewhere mentally! After a few days of blocking thresholds and doorways in the home so that Shiloh would have to wait behind me and step back out of the threshold and let me go first, Shiloh started to learn she did not need to plow out in front and take charge anymore. She could stay back and trust me to lead.

After a week of having a calmer and more structured walk, Shiloh was now able to ignore the everyday noises that used to send her into a frenzy. Shiloh was able to hear children's excited voices playing in their swimming pool across the street without even looking their way. There was no exploding. There was no lunging. There was no flying forward in a tangled rage. She calmly kept walking and even stayed a bit behind me, allowing me to lead and guide her. But wait, how was this possible if I hadn't even worked on her reactivity to people yet? Did providing her with a calmer walk also help calm the areas within her stimulated mind? Absolutely! A calm walk goes hand in hand with a calm mind, which makes the stimuli that the dog is reactive to become less triggering.

From getting calm behavior when I sat down the food dish to calm behavior when putting on her leash, it seemed as if Shiloh was not in fight mode anymore.

Shiloh had been left to free roam her home from the time she was a small puppy (remember our chapter "The Art of Tethering"?). She had lots of windows and doors she could see through and was constantly barking out of the windows and doors at anything and everything that passed by. This kept Shiloh in fight mode 24-7, and she never learned to shut it off. My first recommendation to her owners was to crate train her and not allow her so much freedom. At this time, Shiloh had never learned how to be comfortable in a crate from a young age, so we needed to start crate training her at the age of six years old. It took three full days, but Shiloh learned to go into her crate without freezing and pulling back, and she learned to quietly lie down and feel what stillness felt like. I started increasing her crate time, and eventually she fell asleep inside of it while I washed dishes in the kitchen just a few rooms away. I strongly believe that Shiloh would not have reacted so well to crate training had she and I not first worked on calming her mind during our walks together.

A lot of the time, when I receive board and training jobs, I do not start with obedience training. I do not ask the dog for a lot of demands or give instructions right away. I always start with the walk. Something so simple, but so powerful. A dog that experiences distracting walks likely owns that walk (and the walker). If your dog owns the walk, they own just about everything else at home and outside of the home—including you. Everything you do with one another will likely feel chaotic, and your dog will always be "on." She will never learn to experience peacefulness. Teaching your dog to walk properly solves behavior problems that usually also show up in the home and when out in public. A dog who has been taught to properly walk on the leash, staying calm and a little behind the walker, will prove calmer in the home and more well-behaved during outings to your favorite places. Shiloh had lots of training, and we did not stop with the walk. There was lots of work to do, but our *first* step to success was the walk.

From this point forward, every morning around 6:00 a.m., Shiloh and I had our walk together. We grew closer as a team as I became her source of calmness. We came to trust each other more as we became one on the same leash.

## Chapter 6

# THE REACTIVE MIND (AND WHERE IT COMES FROM)

While there can be a hundred and one different reasons why a dog experiences leash reactivity, 99 percent of the time you can expect that the dog is experiencing some level of insecurity or discomfort.

Around seventeen years ago, when I first started learning about dog training, I was taught what is called the "purely positive training" approach to re-activity. This method is limited only to food-reward-based training. As I discussed in chapter 3, when I first started learning, what I eventually started to realize was that this style of training was the mere approach of shoving hot dogs or turkey in the dog's face to distract them from the feelings they were ex-periencing toward any particular stimuli in that mo-ment, and, well, if the dog was not food motivated, you were completely out of luck. These were the very dogs that were then deemed "untrainable" or "not fit for society and should be put down." I knew there had to be a better way. I knew that this approach was far too limited for the results I wanted to achieve as a dog trainer. I sought to find better approaches.

I eventually met a teacher whose training practices were based more on old-school training methods, which did implement rewards but also used aversions (a.k.a. corrections). His approach was to train a dog's obedience cues to such a high standard that you could then use that obedience to distract the dog from the stimuli. For example, a dog that wants to bark when seeing another dog was taught to go into a heel command where full focus was on the handler. The obedience had to be done at a high level in order to overpower the urge to react. Although blown away by the impact and commitment the obedience training demonstrated, I was not so impressed with the fact that we were not changing the way the dog *felt* about the situation or the stimulus but more so using the obedience as a kind of Band-Aid. Once the dog's obedience had terminated, such as when the dog was released from the command, it then went back to its reactive self, and the feelings of discomfort were still present. I sought out, yet again, another way of obedience training.

I went on to study with a very knowledgeable trainer who focused on how the dog *felt* in certain situations. The training was aimed at healing those feelings of discomfort and insecurity rather than slapping a Band-Aid on them. Let's consider a dog with leash reactivity, whether it be to a person, another dog, or a thing. Instead of correcting the reactivity, find out *why* the reactivity is happening. What is making the dog uncomfortable? From there, determine how to work with those discomforts to a point where the dog can handle increased difficulty as needed. In the previous chapter, I did not try stopping Shiloh's reactivity during our walks. Instead, I used the walk as a time to understand Shiloh and allow her to get to know me as well. Once that bond was established, I was then able to start correcting her reactivity because I understood how she felt and why she was feeling that way.

I like to first teach the dog boundaries. Thresholds are a good place to start when it comes to boundaries, such as with a dog that likes to bolt out of the doorway or does not know how to back off something they want. Teaching an "out" or "leave it" command as well as threshold boundaries (teaching the dog to back off or away at thresholds) along with walking manners is your key starting point for good manners.

But total rehabilitation must change the discomfort the dog feels in that situation. If your dog has learned that barking or lunging gets rid of that discomfort, well, then why not do it? We must show them there is no reason for an outburst, and if they are feeling uncomfortable or want more space from the other person or dog, they can tell us politely and choose another way to communicate, such as turning their head away from the oncoming stimuli, sniffing the ground, or gathering behind you. When your dog is doing these things to signal discomfort to you, you must make sure you notice and are paying attention to your dog's cues and signals.

For example, sometimes when walking past another dog or person, our dog may shift to the right side of us after being taught to walk only on the left side. Your dog is likely shifting sides to create a bubble and more space so that he or she is not so close to whatever is making them feel uncomfortable. Instead of seeing this as our dog's cutoff signal, we instinctively jerk our dog back to the left side and think they are being disobedient for crossing sides. Another example of your dog offering you a cutoff cue is when he or she begins sniffing the ground when an oncoming dog or person approaches. A mistake people often make is that instead of giving the dog more space, they let the other walker approach with their hyperactive dog. Now your dog says, "Well, I tried to tell ya! Next time, I think exploding will work better." Dogs are remarkable creatures, always communicating with us if we just listen. I believe my job as a dog trainer is to train the owner first. I must teach the owner their dog's signals and how to read those signals. This will set the owner up for long-term success. If I train a dog and not the owner, then once that dog returns home, it will eventually revert to its old ways because I haven't taught the owner anything.

Once you have taught your dog impulse control with "out" or "leave" commands, polite manners at doorways, and respecting special pressure, you can start mixing in the stimulus they are reactive to. I like to start with a good distance, allowing the dog to be successful at first. Use your social pressure to "own" the space in front of the dog and the stimuli. Increasing distances to be closer with patience and time, you can work on passing by the actual stimuli. Create scenarios like real-life walks in your own controllable areas first before venturing out into the real world where anything can happen! Don't try to rush this phase, as setting the dog up for success during the beginning stages is key. The more they do it right, the more they can practice and learn to do it correctly. If all they've ever known is to bark, or lunge or do both when faced with these particular stimuli, then that's all they have practiced and learned, and it will take time to undo that in their brains. You are essentially rewiring your dog's brain! Have several sessions of success before trying to move closer to the stimuli or creating new challenges for the dog. If your dog used to react thirty feet away from the stimuli and now you've gotten the dog to be OK from thirty feet away, then do this many different times before expecting to get closer. Things like keeping distance, getting someone to help you, and finding the right dog (if your dog is leash reactive to dogs) to help can all be part of the challenge, and this is why it's very helpful to hire a good trainer who has this set up already. I can usually get a dog far along before the owner has to take over, which therefore makes the owner's job so much easier!

Another good concept that I have had a lot of success with (if we're going to get more advanced here) is adding the "e-collar and moving back" trick. This has worked well with most every dog I've trained using this technique. The concept consists of you conditioning the dog to the e-collar by first finding their level. This means finding where the dog "feels" the e-collar but where it's not too high to make the dog scared or very uncomfortable. You can do this by putting the e-collar on and starting on level one. Then, start pressing the stem button as you slowly dial up. Continue to dial up until the dog does something different from what they were doing before you pressed the button to check, "What was that?" For example, if your dog is sniffing the ground and you press the stem on level six and all the sudden your dog's ears twitch, his head turns, he looks to the air, and so on, then you're ready to begin the technique!

Start this technique by walking forward with the e-collar remote in hand. Start in a distraction-free area first. Let the dog get a little ahead of you, and when they do, move back while pressing the level you identified on the e-collar. The dog will be encouraged to follow you (make sure you are moving back in a backward motion; do not turn your back to the dog and walk away; you must be walking backward facing the dog) and repeat several times without a stimulus present. After doing this several times to where you're almost stepping back, and the dog seems to understand to follow consistently, you can add your "here" or "come" command.

The sequence should look as follows: Walk forward. The dog gets ahead. Press e-collar (on continuous mode). Move back while saying, "Here." When the dog comes next to you, stop pressing the e-collar. The concept is that when the dog is far away, the e-collar communicates something unwanted out in nowhere land (away from you), and when the dog is close, the e-collar goes away to communicate that safety is where you are!

Your e-collar shouldn't be just any e-collar. Try purchasing a mini-educator from e-collar technologies or a Dogtra device. These tools must be the right ones in order to work well. Your e-collar comes with several modes. One of the modes will be "continuous," and this is the one you will use for this exercise. After several days of doing this without a distraction or stimulus, you then want to bring in a distraction, such as another dog or person. Start from a distance where your dog is likely to react well (set them up for success). The moment your dog makes notice of the distraction, press the e-collar and say, "Here," and then move back quickly. Once the dog comes, rinse and repeat. Do this several days at this same distance with success before having the distraction move any closer. Once you have mastered this, you can then move toward the stimuli that cause your dog to react. Repeat the same concept.

I shouldn't fail to mention that what you do in between the training sessions is very important. Say your dog is reactive and you're working on distance reps and have had great success at twenty feet away from a stranger, but then, after training, you are home with the dog and have a delivery, and the FedEx delivery comes to the door and your dog is lost—and now they are too close. EXPLOSION! And then we get set back and now feel discouraged. You must always keep in mind your dog's training program and that you're forever in that mode. Don't think that training is over after a training session. The training that is most crucial is what happens in daily life and routine. Remember, training is lifelong and should be part of our routines with our dogs, not just when wearing the training bag!

# Chapter 7

# YOUR DOG IS NOT AN ASSHOLE

I often hear from dog owners that their dog is a jerk, an asshole, acting like a brat, or is being revengeful. For example, "My dog pees on purpose just because I left him alone" or "My dog always bites at his leash when I'm just trying to take him for a walk" or "My dog bites at my ankles when I'm just trying to feed her." These are all common complaints I have heard from my clients, but ask yourself: Is it that your dog is a brat, or have YOU taught your dog that this behavior is acceptable?

Let's look at OUR behaviors in these examples.

When we interact with our dogs, we are usually encouraging either unwanted behaviors or wanted behaviors. For example, your puppy looks so cute when jumping up and down and barking and whining for their food when meals are served. Puppies do this for several weeks without any feedback that their behavior is wrong. Your little puppy then turns six months old and is barking, demanding their meals, jumping up on the counters (because now they can reach them), spilling things over, jumping on you—the list goes on. We hire a trainer and complain that the dog is out of control. We go for a walk, and the dog likes to bite his leash, which looks kind of funny and cute as he tries to walk himself, so we do nothing. Then the dog grows into this habit, and it becomes annoying as now the behavior has probably grown more intense, and the dog is basically playing tug of war with the leash as you try to go for what you had hoped to be a pleasurable walk. Another example is bolting out of the door. We are often rushing to work or school, and our dog needs to be walked before we can leave. Bolting out the door and pulling on the leash for the walk are then inevitable. Now one day the leash breaks or slips, and the dog is loose, bolting out the door—what he thinks is normal—while we scream and yell to get him back. We then hire a trainer and say, "My dog doesn't listen and runs away any chance they get." In other words, "My dog is a jerk," but in fact, we are the ones who taught them that this behavior is acceptable.

Let's look at a more serious behavior nuisance, such as reactivity. Oftentimes, dogs are reactive to another person or another dog to create more space between what is uncomfortable to them, as we talked about in chapter 6. Because the dog is barking and lunging and looks like a madman, the other person or the other dog will cross the street, turn around, or go the other way. Sometimes it is mostly we who might do this, trying to avoid the situation or embarrassment—so the dog learns the only way to create space and get rid of the stimuli is to act like a roaring lion. If we don't pay attention to our dog's signals when uncomfortable and can only understand there is an issue when the dog reacts and goes into a full-blown explosion, then the dog will learn that's the only way to get you to understand how they're feeling. The dog is not being an asshole for acting like a raging lunatic, for we have taught this.

It is important to know and understand that almost all things our dogs do come from some sort of teaching on our end. It is important to know that often we don't understand our canine companions and don't pick up on their signals of communication, often resulting in dog fights or explosions. Only then do we see there's a problem. Another popular one is "My dog is being spiteful." "He only pees when I leave him alone because he's mad at me." This is a common misconception. Dogs do not contemplate how to get back at their owners for leaving them alone or taking their favorite toy or treat away. Dogs react to learned behavior or when feeling discomfort. Again, in this example, the dog is feeling discomfort and stress. When a dog is stressed or overwhelmed, this can cause soiling, even when they are all but potty trained normally. Dogs with separation anxiety are often potty trained on a daily routine basis, but when left alone, they resort straight to elimination in the house. This is a stress response and not a potty training issue. Your dog is not being an asshole because he feels discomfort.

Think about everything you do and what it is teaching your dog. If my dog barks or demands their food, I wouldn't prep the food faster just to get him quiet and then give an unruly dog their biggest reward in life—FOOD! If your puppy or dog is barking for food, simply put it back and walk away for a few minutes before trying again. You may want to teach your dog a good "down" or "sit and wait" or a place command to teach the dog that calmly waiting earns the food, not the demanding noise such as barking or excessive whining.

Teaching your dog to wait at the doorway before going for a walk can help avoid plunging out the doorways, resulting in too much pulling on a walk. Your wait command and working on impulse control help in many scenarios.

If your dog is showing behaviors that you do not like, then don't continue to walk, feed, or play in response to that behavior. I like to teach what I call replacement behaviors. For example, if my dog likes to jump for the tug toy and I don't want this, I can replace it with teaching a sit or wait cue to get the toy. If my dog is lunging out the doorways, I can teach them to stay back when approaching thresholds—stepping back and waiting earns the walk. Just keep in mind what you're doing in response to the dog's behavior, and be mindful that we are always teaching them something, whether it is good or bad.

A lot of the unwanted "bad behaviors" we see in our pet dogs are caused by our lack of understanding and teaching. Our dogs are not being revengeful, spiteful, or "assholes."

# Chapter 8

# SOCIALIZATION— WHAT PEOPLE THINK IT IS AND WHAT IT IS NOT

As humans, we know that it is normal for kids to go to school, socialize, make friends, and so on. We think that because children have social groups (whether through school, day care, or the like), the same must apply to our dogs. One of the most common things I get from clients is that they cannot figure out why their dog doesn't do well in their local dog park or at a day care facility with other dogs. They think something is wrong with their dog and that "all dogs should be social and friendly." Shouldn't they?

I personally love people and socializing, at least for a certain amount of time. But eventually, I need quiet time alone. After all, socialization can be exhausting! There are those who are more introverted, those who may be withdrawn from big crowds and loud noises. There are also those who prefer to keep to themselves, preferring to work on a piece of electronic equipment, write a book, or solve a puzzle while keeping to themselves. There is nothing wrong with any of these personalities. With our dogs, we must remember that it is the same thing. There are different types of "socializing" your dog may enjoy or not enjoy, and that is OK.

But it is important to know what your dog can handle and for how long. Not every dog is suitable for a day care environment where there are many different dogs in one group playing throughout the day without any breaks to be alone in between. Some day cares may also have new or inexperienced staff who do not know how to properly read body language and canine communication and therefore cannot read the signs a fight might break out. You want to do your research on a facility very thoroughly before just dropping your dog off there. You want to evaluate the experience the staff has and how they run their day cares. Some may even allow you to request how often your dog gets a social break. Some let you choose walks in between playtime if your dog requires more exercise. If your dog does not feel comfortable in a huge crowd of other dogs, opt for the walking choices only. Social crowds in places like dog parks can be very risky. You don't know who's coming in or what they react to. Usually, in a dog park environment, there is no monitoring of who plays with whom, for how long, or in what way. This makes it a very hard environment in which to train properly. There shouldn't be toys or food involved in large social groups of dogs, as is usually the case at dog parks. This is just asking for trouble. There are plenty of ways for your dog to exercise and have fun without throwing him into the lion's den.

It's very important to keep in mind that our dogs can be social creatures and behave well around other dogs without day care or dog parks. Training your dog around other dogs is a great way to teach him or her in an environment of distractions while still allowing exposure to socialization. Teaming up with someone you are close to whose dog you know well is another safe way to get the dog-to-dog exposure if that's what you're looking for. Keep in mind that if your dog isn't the type to enjoy being in large play-groups and is pressured by the wrong dog or has a bad experience, you can actually do more harm than good by forcing large playgroups onto each other.

Socialization can be a touchy subject because almost everyone has a different idea of what that should entail or mean. To me, if my dog can be neutral around other dogs who may be acting rowdy or barking at him, can listen well when given any obedience cue around however many dogs confront us, walks without dragging when seeing another dog go for a walk, then he is a well socialized and trained dog to me! I don't need him to play and run around in a park because, again, you never know who may be in that group, and the temperaments or mannerisms may not be something you want your dog influenced by in the first place. I've seen more dog fights in dog parks than I have seen friendships made in dog parks. Just be wise and use good judgment when it comes to your dog's socialization, and know your dog well enough to know what he can and cannot deal with and for how long. An excellent way to give your dog socialization safely and effectively doesn't always involve them running off the leash in a room or bench with twenty or thirty other dogs. Sometimes (and in most cases), great socialization comes from just working your dog around other dogs they can see. For example, I'll take my dog for a walk, and every time we encounter another dog walking by, we might practice our heeling walk, down stays, focus on me drills, or sit stays. If your dog thinks other dogs just mean "play" all the time, this can cause you to lack the focus and obedience control most of us want when faced with other distractions like another dog in the first place. Whenever I'm out and about with one of my dogs, whether we be at a store, public park, restaurant, etc., I'm always asked, "How do you get such great attention from your dogs? It's like they don't even care what's going on around them. Other dogs are even barking at them, and they don't seem to care." Bingo! Exactly, and I didn't get this from any dog park.

In conclusion, socialization means a lot of things. In most cases, it's different in everyone's opinion. What is socialization to you, and why? If my dog listens and focuses on me when we are out in public places, and if fifteen dogs are lunging and barking and mine sit calmly attentive to me, I call this a very well exposed (and social) dog. I call this "socialized."

*    *    *

After reading this book, I hope you can see the big differences you can make in your dog's life by implementing some of the tips and guides in this book to help you better understand why your dog may be doing or not doing some of the things you struggle with. I hope this book can encourage you and give you insight on how to successfully work with your dog and apply training as part of your daily lives together.

Thank you for reading, and happy training!

Milton Keynes UK
Ingram Content Group UK Ltd.
UKHW040741261123
433299UK00001B/1

9 798822 924024